10/15/07

Alice —

I'm very grateful for all the help you've given me with my poems over the years. Your gift as a poet and your dedication as a writer have been an inspiration to me. I hope you'll accept this little book in the spirit of fun and play in which it is intended.

Ed

One Hundred Famous Views of Edo

Doug MacPherson
& Edward Smallfield

Battery Press
Berkeley, California

Book design by Philip Krayna Design, www.pkdesign.net.

ISBN 0-97230-210-7. Library of Congress Control Number: 2003-106927.

Published by Battery Press, 2466 Hilgard Avenue #205, Berkeley CA 94709.

I wish to thank Maria Manurung for believing in me; Mom, Dad, Kathleen and Ann for their support; Mary Ellen Brown, Robert Neblett, Chris West; all my coworkers at GHCP for coming to hear me read; David Harrison Horton, Denise Newman and Laura Walker for their thoughtful readings of this book; my fellow poets in the workshop where the germ of this work began; Valerie Coulton and Steve Hemenway for their enthusiasm and editing; and Ed, my mentor. —Doug MacPherson

I want to thank Doug for his unflagging enthusiasm, energy and creativity in the pursuit of this project, Steve for his support and dedication as a reader and editor, and Valerie for everything. —Edward Smallfield

prologue sato dairi

detached
palace
literally village palace

used by imperial consorts
sometimes inhabited
by emperors

i auction

each print's cost
vibrates in the seller's voice

here you can buy a boy
or a girl
for the same price

the geisha's mats
bright by moon milk

or these bottles of sake
you can't drink from

can't be what you pay for

ii Murasaki Shikibu

pretty
yet shy
unsociable
fond of old tales
conceited
so wrapped up
in poetry
spitefully
looking down

iii value price cost

Or, as James Joyce once said
of *Lady Chatterley's Lover,*

I hear you can get
the real thing
for the same price.

iv ronin

in feudal Japan

lordless
wandering
samurai

outlaw

v Murasaki Shikibu (ii)

i really am
strangely gentle
quite unlike
what you
had been led
to believe

my nature
is
as it is

vi day job

in your notebook
this list:
alarm
solar panel
door opener
chair rail
exterior ramp
button on front door

vii ikiryo

evil spirit
of a living
person
haunts people
without conscious
knowledge
of the owner

viii button on front door

She drops her kimono.
The female sexual organ is gorgeous.

ix torn lantern

the kimono lies
where it fell
her scent
embroiders
the sash

x the subject of all poems is the clock

A skein of geese unwinds the sky.
Hiroshige fills the harbor with sails.

No fireworks tonight
except under this table,
your lit fuse.

xi the subject of all poems is the cock

super
imposed
text
on this bonsai scene

he sees in words
understands emotion
spirituality
in a word
that rises
yes
in the sand
yes

xii yes

yes
yes
she blooms
he jerks
back
turned

xiii aesthetics

Of course this room is empty.

Only the shadow of her hair,
her neck,
the back of her kimono
behind the screen.

xiv on the floor

ten bamboo
aren't green
anymore

brown stalks
browner joints

grow like weeds

xiv.i Murasaki Shikibu (iii)

not betrothed
until the advanced
age of
twenty

xv closing time

Today the yen sinks below 120.
The euro avoids dollar parity.

xvi good golly miss

They fired a bunch
today because the Pacific rim
economy took a hit.

xvii conception

fireworks
in such detail
above the harbor
littered with boats
high bright
candle wilts
sad
as a penis
after
remembers
hands
on knees
under tables

xviii whole truth

You try not to speculate
on the bus about the trial.

you imagine her
protest
smeared cow
blood
ruddies
cheeks

I'm guilty, your honor.

xix Oz

Do you dream
in color, she asks,
or black and white,
then answers herself
without a pause
for breath, me,
I only dream
in purple, you know,
like Ellington says,
in my deep purple reverie,
and I notice that her tongue glows,
purple, and her finger
nails, and her lips,
purple, purple, purple,
a shade darker
than her violet
eyes, and the old lady
with the broom
sweeps, sweeps, sweeps
the drunk's lost coins
and the drunk's lost fingers
and her purple hands
already pocket
her change and my change,
her fingers and my fingers,
my tongue and my toenails and my eyes.

xx French Riviera

You know as well
as I do that this necklace
is a fake.

Well I'm not.

xxi le samouraï

in a French movie
because all movies are French
angel lips and gangster eyes
shot entirely in pastels
never changes
expression
as the actor ages
once gorgeous
as a boxer
in fifties Italy

his face a book of loss

xxii French Riviera (ii)

white dress
black tux
his sad penis
her dying embers

xxii.i me and my Lomo (Mathias Fiegl)

How will they look when I put a hat on their head and shoot them five times from the hip from above with the flash in my other hand on the street in the hotel in a car in a bar? The Chinese love Lomo they are fun people who like to be shot with a foreigner's camera they play with you they laugh with you. Five days in Hong Kong I met more and more the rhythm of the city and the rhythm of shooting Lomo feed on each other. People have a Lomo look.

xxii.ii Lomo look

Lomo Embassy Tokyo
www.lomo.com/Japan

xxiii Roman numerals

Buddhists count
by weeds
by waves
by wind

one
just
one

xxiv anatomically correct

fuses
and after
the rocket
this reddish
residue
hazy
and menstrual
sun setting
on the bay
sails
as you read
his prints
so exact
you know
the shape
of those knees
naked
under the table

xxv sold

for the same price
a boy
menstrual blood
on his lip
vibrating
geisha's milk
mats the hair

xxvi residue

sad
as a man
after

xxvii trumpet from Paris

penis sets
before sunrise
matted
sticky
folds against her
a spoon

xxviii trumpet

polishes
these stars
this moon

these nipples
sore
with scouring

xxix Paris

Miles Davis
dead in the newspaper
in Helen's poem.

Those French words
somehow too soft.

Me, on my bridge, listening
to Amiri Baraka's elegy.

The name of the exit.

A flare on the street.
An accident.

xxx clue

i suspect
Colonel Mustard
in *la salle à manger*
with the knife
no the library
la bibliothèque
before dawn
before laying
it down

xxxi what I mean is

you can hear it
that trumpet
in these Japanese prints

lies down
on this geisha's
green mats

listen

xxxii listen

you can hear

spit and sand
sand and spit
polishing

this moon's nipples

xxxii.i Murasaki Shikibu (iv)

clandestinely
teaching
her mistress

xxxii.ii great wave off Kanagawa

blind rowers
pile of blankets
skulls
reabsorb water
reaching
like kale

xxxii.iii waves off Bolinas

Hawaiian shirts
fit like death's
loose grip

look for a cig
ignore the bitch
in white boots
who screams
in a frying pan
warmed by a ghost

xxxii.iv listen again

she screams sand
in a pan
teeth grit
to gums

xxxii.v thunderstorm at Ōhashi (arithmetic)

four men
on eight legs

(arachnid)

run
through this
storm

(as if to arrive
somewhere)

cold rain
hot sweat

stew
in their own
broth

xxxii.vi thunderstorm at Ōhashi (process)

those men
blurred (almost)
in their haste

and his haste
to record

and our haste
to

xxxii.vii thunderstorm at Ōhashi (image)

a bridge across

on the river a boat

xxxiii 33

he fell three
times
knees
broken
his throat
can't taste
what the mouth
knows

xxxiv church & state

for Christians
that number
33

in Japan
Shinto
Buddhism

shaved heads
chrysanthemums
bells

do you believe?
a monkey's DNA
98 percent mine

98 percent yours

xxxv garden in Kameido

Just this crotch,
cropped, black and bare,
and these few blossoms,
bright as popcorn.

xxxvi garden in Kameido (ii)

a geisha strolls under blossoms
with an American sailor
who tells her all about Oz

xxxvii haiku

It doesn't matter if she wears purple or red.
She kissed me and that's enough.
5   7   5
Let's begin with one syllable: *Oz*.

xxxviii garden in Kameido (iii)

Her pale hand lights
his purple fuse.

xxxix garden in Kameido (iv)

this crotch
this black
branch

a sign
the lovers stroll
under

xl garden in Kameido (v)

Maybe these lovers aren't lovers.

Maybe these aren't lovers
are just before love,
or just after.

xli garden in Kameido (vi)

Just before love.
Just after.

Popcorn
on a black branch.

xli.i Murasaki Shikibu (v)

the color of
your name
wisteria
fragrant
after a word
a branch
your lips

xlii garden in Kameido (vii)

In this country without alphabet
a few black branches
arranged and rearranged
bare as crotches.

xlii.i alphabet

there's not an alphabet
that survived man
your iteration
is Dutch

kamu is to you
as i to me
and for that
all i can
remember
are the corners
of your eyes

xliii garden in Kameido (viii)

these lovers eat:
clams
mussels
octopus
squid
sea slugs

xliv garden in Kameido (ix)

He prepares her
with miso and ginger
and a little sake.

She prefers him
with just a little sea salt.

xlv garden in Kameido (x)

Each country
flies a flag
sings an anthem.

Each lover throws
the uniform away,
if only for an hour.

xlv.i Murasaki Shikibu (vi)

more adept at
memorizing
Chinese characters
than her brother

xlvi patriotism

These sea slugs just don't seem
Japanese.

xlvii patriotism (ii)

Nor do these transparent frogs
whose guts you can read
in this light.

xlviii patriotism (iii)

How do I love thee?
Let me count the ways
with one hand clapping.

xlix patriotism (iv) or the Saturn

hate these
fucking
ads
don't care

if they're teasers
they're stupid

What country are you from?

I new hope

Unlike swimmers, unexhausted,
these lovers kiss.

Hell, the war is over.
What's to fear?

This might be my father,
my mother, or yours.

Freshly pressed, his uniform sparkles.
His sergeant's bars kiss the sun.

Ii platform

His sergeant's ass kisses sun.
He holds his brag and his girl,
wraps arms around shoulders,
kind of like a man's, he thinks.

lii new hope (ii)

Both high heels high off the platform
she kisses and kisses and kisses.

That old couple in dark cloth–
my grandparents, yours?–smiles with approval.

Hell, the war is over.
Let them fuck on the platform.

All night iron wheels kiss iron rails.
Kiss, kiss, kiss.

liii new hope (iii)

On this honeymoon she names
native flowers all night.

Dogwood, mountain laurel.
Spring in North Carolina.

This morning
he forgets to shave.

Americans gave chocolate bars to starving kids.
I was one of them, he reminds her.
Death is the mother of beauty,
he whispers, just before dawn.

Hell, the war is over.

liv riot

That we had gone to stop the war. At the concert, the night before, making towards the stage because Travis knew the bassist. A soft carpet of bodies entirely covering that enormous lawn. Trying to pick our way between: no place to set foot that wasn't flesh. If only we had read the dictionary: a disturbance consisting of wild and turbulent conduct of a large number of persons, as a mob. In our minds, we were the opposite, each individual exercising his individual rights as an individual. A soft carpet of bodies. If we had let ourselves lie down, that morning, on the road. If every molecule in a glass of water should decide to jump in the same direction at once. Something spilled. On the floor. Mop it up. Yes, somebody is always there to mop it up.

lv le samouraï (ii)

Somebody
to mop it up.

A samurai.

lvi after

There had been a war but it was over. Our mothers and fathers lit cigarettes with silver lighters. The target on the Lucky box. Somebody poured everybody a highball. Bourbon and ginger ale. A wall is a good thing: either you stand on one side or the other. Some of those singers wore plaid shirts. Will the circle be unbroken? A wall is a good thing. To be on one side or the other of. Stand on top, and somebody shoots you.

lvii le samouraï (iii)

in French
(because all movies
are French)
pale eyes
pistols
pastels
shot in
this blue
as if the color
of his eyes
leaks

lvii.i le samouraï (iv)

every week he asks
her to play dominoes
insists she drink red
wine he calls out
his wife's name
from bed

losing books
of memory

lvii.ii le samouraï (v)

somebody throws
a window
open

to seep
the morning
in

or the night

out

lviii Biwa Ko

Tradition says Murasaki began a novel
in a temple on the shores of this lake.

lix and that novel began

    Hell, this war is over.

lx Murasaki's lake

    at dawn
    water the color
    of semen
    of pearls

    what she wears

lx.i the color of the air

    in the hour between
    waking and
    sleep

    and

    and

lxi Hikaru Genji

shining prince

son of the Old Emperor
and concubine Kiritsubo

male beauty
male charm

lxii male beauty

a little boy runs
through wet grass
skin the color of polished bronze

lxiii male charm

a little boy runs
through the shallow river
his thing clangs
polished bronze

lxiv Murasaki Shikibu (vii)

her diary
does not mention
him
nor does it
refer
to their children

lxiv.i In a

*certain reign (whose can it have been?) someone of no very
great rank, among all his Majesty's Consorts and Intimates,
enjoyed exceptional favor.*

lxiv.ii mother

styling Takane Sugimoto
makeup Hiramoto
hair Akino
model Asami Imajuku

gathered shirt
chiffon pleated skirt
pleated apron
wooden sandals

lxiv.iii mother mujōkan (impermanence)

too painful
to write
about what's not
named
or maybe
too not
painful

lxv Kiritsubo no Koi

literally paulownia tub
mother of Hikaru Genji
persecuted
by other court
ladies
died
at an early age

lxvi Mushi Mezuru Himegimi

one of ten
stories
the lady
who loved
insects

lxvii proper names

> pronounce correctly
> with reverence
> as you would want
> your own
> after your ashes

lxviii your name

> Don't say it.
> Just don't say it.

lxix 69

> improper
> she said
> naming
> the thing

lxx improper names

> with reverence
> in silence

lxxi Murasaki Shikibu (viii)

scribble scribble scribble

her brush tip
swollen with ink

as beautiful as

or her own
engorged with

lxxi.i the pleasure

of lying
in bed
and writing

lxxi.ii the pleasure (ii)

of lying
in bed
and

lxxii scribble scribble

scribble scrabble
doom sturm drang
tip of
her brush
engorged
a hand full of electrons
an appendage
traces

the swing
of this
pendulum

lxxiii Dear Doug

Yes, the hidden tower.

Don't worry.
It's plenty disturbing enough.

lxxiv All things are tragic when a mother watches

as Frank O'Hara knew,
and said,
though not very often.

lxxv I rode like a god when the mare reared

but that was in another country
and besides, the horse is dead.

lxxvi yet another festival

something to do with lanterns
or moons

because these lanterns hang
moonlike

here
above our heads

her hand also
somehow lunar

in this light
charred stone or ash

lit by
reflected sun

lxxvii moon festival

> or
> a couple
> of American
> kids
> in a car

lxxviii Dear Doug (ii)

> Look at this one.
> Those fireworks again.
>
> Each flare
> bright as a fuse.
>
> His hand on her sash.
> Scent of her kimono on this boat's deck.
>
> What he might have said.
> A translation of a translation.

lxxix lovers (Utamaro)

the perfect lovers
wear no faces

only his topknot
the back of her neck

this slice
of her ass

define her
a patch

pale thigh
fully clothed

or almost
his cock

cooks
in her oven

lxxx lovers (Utamaro ii)

yes, Doug, it is always just
algebra,
her naked ass
and bare patch
of thigh
commutative
and associative
across parentheses
and garments
along his

lxxxi lovers (Utamaro iii)

or maybe chemistry
that's the word

in those novels
that sell lots of copies

let's write like that
make money

his carbon her dioxide
her neon and his

neon is an inert gas
and won't burn

but brightens
when a current

shakes
his electrons

lxxxii lovers (Utamaro iv)

autopsy:
scalpel, doctor,
clamp,
or, as your old song says—

I fall in love too easily

lxxxiii lovers (Utamaro v)

attention
coordination:

that she should manage
her fan
while he fucks her

lxxxiii.i Tamakazura

and that novel went on
pushing her inkstone
so moved by things
a branch of plum blossom
vanishing dew from
eyebrows

she copied text
she just read

lxxxiv hackers

> put to death
> for wired money
> shamed
> hired language

lxxxv balancing act

> you want this box
> your pale face
> your pits for eyes
> arms and legs
> shrivel a hold
> like kale
> on a branch

lxxxvi like kale

> as if to say
> the cabbageness
> of reaching
>
> look long enough
> kale becomes blue
> like waves

lxxxvii this shade of blue

further from bay
eyes with that t-shirt
drool on your sleeping bag
spray on my face

lxxxviii far from bay

everything's water
if you look long enough

lxxxviii.i bottled water

photography Simon
text Mitsuru Hayakawa

Ryal Watson once called
human beings
walking water
60 percent
of our body
is water
bottles made of skin
skins full of water
everything around us
a sponge

lxxxix this is one

Van Gogh copied

before Gauguin
before the ear

on Alan's wall
a copy of a copy of a copy

how skinny
these men
on a bridge
under the rain

skinny maybe
skinny as the Master
years later
at Arles

xc the old man listens

to Monk
hour after hour
usually a gay one
Lulu's Back in Town
or maybe Ellington
Mood Indigo
Black and Tan Fantasy
on a luminous afternoon
in late summer
each note
a drop of iodine
stains the sun

xci the great wave

this ocean sweats
and the men
in this boat
barely visible
under the swells
also sweat
salty and cold
enough to drown in

the sweat
a woman
sweats
while she waits
for her lover

xcii always

we seem to be looking
back
to these fire
works
or up

our eyes
can't see
what our hands
play at
mostly
boats drifting
and fuses

xciii a conspiracy of angels

To one a house is given.
To another a room.

To plan
or plot.

A plot of land.
Just enough to be buried on.

xciv a conspiracy of hours

Beaded together.
A rosary.

The genes conspire this organism.

DNA
splits and spins,
stutters.

xcv you the rock

So this year I'm aiming to cut an album and perform overseas. Asia, New York, the Bronx, nonstop. I wanna see how far I can go, you know, 'cause there ain't any Japanese performing like that. I wanna change the minds of people who think of Japanese as these meek, slicked back, parted hair, glasses wearing creatures. I wanna say, a Japanese can look like this too! We got the funk!

xcvi soya fresh source

chocolate soy wonder my
sidekick kawabanga
ninja free up shut 'em down
type 2 bulletproof chainlink
shirts baseball style
ninja balaclava
Motorola microtac 207
style stop desender
process evolution of soy

xcvii Murasaki Shikibu (ix)

If only you were
a boy
how happy
I should be.

xcviii Murasaki Shikibu (x)

scribble scribble
scribble scrabble

brush tip
swollen

with ink
as beautiful as

her own
engorged

xcix happy sad

we love you P5
oh yes we do
we love you P5
i may be true
when you're not near to us
we're blue
oh P5 we love you

xcix.i Murasaki Shikibu (xi)

inkstick stuck in
whose words
whose Genji

c I fell in love just once
(and it had to be with you)

Always, in Japanese prints,
some reference to
a young boy's knees.

Poetry is a human art.
Throat, gauze, puncture.
Penance.

Begin again.

notes on process

ES: For a long time I had been caught in an idea of my poems as "my language," "my work," and the collaborative process broke down that notion into a freer and more open approach to writing.

DM: The collaborative aspects helped me generate material and deal with the found language I was collecting.

ES: Part of the pleasure of the project was responding to what you had written without pretending that I understood. I thought misunderstandings would produce as much poetry as understandings.

DM: It felt like a dialogue and at the same time private conversations in our own heads that our material triggered in each other.

ES: Echoing was very important in both the process and product of the work. You started that when you changed "the subject of all poems is the clock" to "the subject of all poems is the cock."

DM: I never expected we'd get something so cohesive. The repetition of titles and echoing helped that a lot.

ES: The cohesion that arose is one of the results that changed my aesthetic. I realized that you don't have

to search for cohesion. If you keep writing, cohesion
will find you.

– – –

ES: The idea of writing one hundred pieces to match
Hiroshige's number of paintings of Edo was a huge part of
the inspiration for me. The idea that we would write "lots
of pieces" seemed to necessitate a certain pace or speed
or haste. I figured we could throw away any pieces that
didn't work.

DM: And that made the revision process interesting in
trying to figure out how to sort out the pieces and where
they should fall together.

ES: It was like a puzzle with diverse solutions. I felt that the
pieces all fit together, and that they could fit together in
multiple ways. So the final manuscript feels provisional,
but also right.

DM: I remember knowing the last piece, which is yours,
would be the final piece because the tone seemed right.
But you wrote that early on or in the middle of the process.

– – –

DM: I'm not sure how we decided when we were finished.
We gathered a lot of material and decided at one point to
meet and edit what we put together. It was a process that
we were developing and learning.

ES: In some ways no book of poems is ever finished.
I felt that we had "enough." So it seemed that putting the
book together was the thing to do, rather than writing
new pieces.

DM: I never thought about it being a book. I've never really
thought of my work or poetry in those terms up until now.
It's hard for me to connect things sometimes, especially
when I'm in the midst of creating.

ES: In some ways, the act of creation and the published
work function in separate universes.

DM: But if we just speak in terms of the work being
"finished" (not necessarily publishable), I do have the
experience of knowing when I've finished a poem. And
with Edo I didn't have that feeling as strongly.

ES: For me, the feeling of being finished varies from
poem to poem. But I don't get a sense of finishing a book.
That usually feels more arbitrary. I really believe that we
could write an indefinite number of Edo pieces.

DM: What we've done, not just the end result but
the process itself, is still speaking to me and will for a
long time.

source notes

prologue sato dairi: Ivan Morris *(The World of the Shining Prince: Court Life in Ancient Japan)*.

i: Hiroshige.

ii: Ivan Morris.

iii: James Joyce (in conversation).

iv: Ivan Morris.

v: Ivan Morris.

vii: Ivan Morris.

viii: Jack Spicer ("For Joe," *Admonitions*).

x: Charles Wright ("Portrait of the Artist with Hart Crane," *The Southern Cross*), Hiroshige.

xiv.i: Ivan Morris.

xvii: Hiroshige.

xix: Ellington – Mills – Bigard ("Mood Indigo").

xx: Alfred Hitchcock *(To Catch a Thief)*.

xxi: Jean-Pierre Melville *(Le Samouraï)*, Luchino Visconti *(Rocco and His Brothers)*.

xxii.i-xxii.ii: *Tokion*, issue no. 12 (the flow issue).

xxiv: Hiroshige.

xxxii.i: Ivan Morris.

xxxii.ii: Hokusai.

xxxii.v–xxxii.vii: Hiroshige.

xxxv–xxxvi: Hiroshige.

xxxviii–xli: Hiroshige.

xli.i: Ivan Morris.

xlii, xliii-xlv: Hiroshige.

xlv.i: Ivan Morris.

xlvi: Issa.

xlviii: Elizabeth Barrett Browning ("How Do I Love Thee?").

xlix: Unidentified advertising agency.

l–liii: Unidentified photographer.

liii: Wallace Stevens ("Sunday Morning," *Collected Poems*).

lvii: Jean-Pierre Melville *(Le Samouraï)*.

lviii: Ivan Morris.

lxi: Ivan Morris.

lxiv: Ivan Morris.

lxiv.i: Murasaki Shikibu *(The Tale of Genji)*.

lxiv.ii: *Tokion*, issue no. 12 (the flow issue).

lxiv.iii–lxvi: Ivan Morris.

lxxiv: Frank O'Hara ("Poem," *Selected Poems*).

lxxv: Frank O'Hara ("Poem," *Selected Poems*), Christopher Marlowe *(The Jew of Malta)*.

lxxvi: Hiroshige.

lxxviii: Hiroshige.

lxxix–lxxxiii: Utamaro.

lxxxii: Cahn – Styne ("I Fall in Love Too Easily").

lxxxiii.i: Ivan Morris.

lxxxv-lxxxvi: Hokusai.

lxxxviii: Robert Creeley ("Just Friends," *For Love*).

lxxxviii.i: *Tokion*, issue no. 12 (the flow issue).

lxxxix: Hiroshige.

xc: Warren – Dubin ("Lulu's Back in Town"), Ellington – Mills – Bigard ("Mood Indigo"), Ellington – Miley ("Black and Tan Fantasy").

xci: Hokusai.

xcii: Hiroshige.

xcv–xcvi: *Tokion*, issue no. 12 (the flow issue).

xcvii: Ivan Morris.

xcix: Pizzicato Five ("We love Pizzicato Five").

c: Dennis – Adair ("Everything Happens to Me").

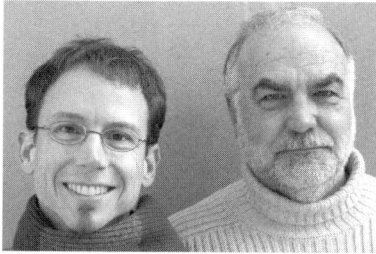

DOUG MACPHERSON
is a poet living in San Francisco. He received honorable mention in the Montalvo Biennial Poetry Competition in winter 2000. His poetry has been published in *Windfall, Fourteen Hills,* and *Rising Waters,* an anthology of poems reflecting on the great flood of 1993. He finished his first short play called *a thousand fathoms* in the fall of 2002, and is pursuing an MFA in Creative Writing at San Francisco State University.

EDWARD SMALLFIELD
is the author of *The Pleasures of C* (Apogee Press, 2001). His poems and stories have appeared in *26, The Battery Review, Fourteen Hills, Manoa, Seven Hundred Kisses, Yellow Silk, ZYZZYVA,* and other periodicals. With Toni Mirosevich and Charlotte Muse, he is the author of *Trio.* He teaches a poetry workshop at University of California at Berkeley Extension.